BRIEF PRAYERS

FOR

BUSY LIVES

10/17

Helen —
Thanks for your friendship.
God Bless you and your family.
Love you,
Pastor

Rev. Dr. John H. Krahn

Rev. Dr. John H. Krahn

krahns@msn.com

Brief Prayers for Busy Lives

All biblical quotations are taken from the New Revised Standard Version.

Additional books are available from Amazon.com or email krahns@msn.com and ask for information on a discounted price.

Library of Congress Cataloging-in-Publication Data is available.

ISBN-13: 9781978005716

ISBN-10: 1978005717

OTHER TITLES BY
JOHN H. KRAHN

Love – It's the Greatest

*Living A Happier Life
At Every Age!*

From Surviving to Thriving -
*A Practical Guide to Revitalize Your
Church*

Seasonings for Sermons III

Washed Any Feet Lately?

Reaching the Inactive Member

Ministry Ideabank

Ministry Ideabank II

Ministry Ideabank III

DEDICATION

This book is dedicated to my Lord Jesus Christ who has loved me unconditionally. It is also dedicated to those people throughout my long life who have loved me and made my life happier. These include my wife, children, grandchildren, sons-in-law, parents, sister, brother-in-law, mother and father-in-law, grandparents, aunts, uncles, cousins, nephews, nieces, mentors, and friends. For each one of them, I am eternally grateful.

CONTENTS

Introduction

There are those days when we all have ten tasks to accomplish and time only to complete five. Even Sundays become full with family activities, sports and household chores. On such hectic days, we often find ourselves praying very little. *Brief Prayers for Busy Lives* is written for these kinds of times.

I am not suggesting that those who read this book need only pray short prayers. During our Lord's very active ministry, he often spent all night in prayer. Activity should never be at the expense of our prayer life. Yet, there are crowded days when we can only grab a few minutes on the run for prayer and consideration.

Whatever in our lives is big enough to worry about, is not too small a thing to pray about. When we pray, we may not always get what we want, but God gives us what we need when we need it. Praying is really an act of worship. For by the act of praying, we are also proclaiming, "It is with you God where I find my refuge and strength."

7

None of the prayers in this book take even a minute to pray. In most cases several can be prayed in a minute. Permit me to suggest you take a few moments each day and allow these brief prayers to inspire your own personal prayers and reflection. Then, even these brief prayers will have a long and beneficial effect on your busy day.

These brief prayers also lend themselves well for use by clergy during public worship along with the prayers of the people. However they are used, may they become a blessing to all who pray them.

I wish to especially thank Charlotte Perreira, Evelyn Andersen Meyers, Jane Kerr, and Dr. Astrid Sipos for doing a careful job of proofreading and making thoughtful suggestions that have improved this book.

ONE

THE LORD'S DAY

First there is that "click,"

    then the music soon followed.

Lord, it did not seem fair

    having to get up so early . . .

      especially on my day off.

I'm glad you helped me get moving.

You know that I enjoy going to church,

    but that extra hour of sleep

      always seems so inviting.

Help me Lord to want to worship you

    more than anything else . . .

      even more than sleep.

It's Sunday, Lord.

I'm really looking forward to church

and to a good sermon.

Yet, when I think about it,

there is much more to church

than the sermon.

On a closer look,

I find other things just as important:

praising you as my Almighty God,

thanking you for forgiving me,

praying for those I love.

Lord, may my worship today

be complete.

And may it also bring a smile

to your face.

It's good, Lord, to be here.

I come to church to be nourished

   with the spiritual food

      of your Word and Sacrament.

My heart and mind feeds

   on these gracious gifts,

      and I am strengthened by them.

Without these gifts,

   I would develop spiritual malnutrition

   which often leads to spiritual death.

Lord, may this never happen to me.

Jesus,

here I am in church again.

Last week certainly was hectic.

Beginning each week with you

    is so very important.

Starting out on the right foot

    makes everything go better.

Assist me, Lord, as I

    hear your Word.

May the Devil neither

    close my ears to your message

    nor tie the tongue of the preacher.

You must be disappointed, Lord.

I just spent the entire church hour

thinking about everything

but you.

Help me turn off

the many distracting thoughts,

so that I may turn on and tune in

only to you.

Next week, I want to offer you

an uninterrupted hour of my worship.

Help me, Lord, to make good

on my intention.

Good Lord,

I heard that the average American

70 years old

will have spent

6 years in eating

11 years working

8 amusing themselves

24 sleeping

5 ½ dressing

3 talking

and only 4 months in church.

When I worship you, Lord,

help me make every minute count.

Gracious Lord,

    you are a full-time God.

You are always on call

    be it in good times,

      bad times,

        or at any time.

I know that you want me

    to be in touch with you

      many times every day.

Help me to realize that

    one hour a week

      really isn't enough.

Thank you, dear Lord

for the weekly opportunity

to attend church.

Unfortunately, millions live in countries

that do not grant this privilege.

Others are unable to attend

because of various issues.

Being able to publicly worship you

is truly a great blessing.

May I never be guilty

of not taking advantage

of this great privilege.

TWO

THE OTHER SIX DAYS

Church was great yesterday, Lord,

    so warm and comfortable.

We even sang hymns that I liked,

    and the sermon was very good.

Now it's back to a messed-up world

    which is often coldly indifferent.

Lord, may some of yesterday's warmth

    be spread into today's world

        through me.

Good morning Lord,

    as another day is beginning,

thank you for yesterday's blessings.

Really Lord, you treated me

    far better than I deserved.

There were those moments

    of which I am not proud.

I am truly grateful that you

    hung in with me.

Accept my heartfelt thanks,

    and may my actions today

        demonstrate my gratitude.

Almighty God,

love is such an abused word.

Used in so many ways,

its meaning is different

for everyone.

Love is an essential word

for your purposes, Lord.

Perhaps an alternative spelling might

better communicate its message.

Give might well do the job . . .

to love means to give oneself to another.

A *for* in front of *give* says it even better . . .

to love means to forgive another.

Lord, help me love by giving.

Help me love by forgiving.

Lord God,

as I move through good and bad times,

may I never lose sight

of that time beyond time . . .

the eternity you made possible.

You gave yourself as a gift for me . . .

one not cheap but ever so costly.

Death by crucifixion.

Life through resurrection.

With you as my Savior,

my ruler,

and my protector,

I know that an eternity of time

will one day be mine.

Dear Lord,

In these days of violence and crime,

we are confronted more and more

with the negative side of existence.

If I could feel your powerful presence

here standing beside me,

I would feel much better.

And yet you are here

and there

and everywhere.

Jesus, I need your strength and direction

as I make my way through life.

With faith and hope, I call upon you,

and patiently welcome your peace.

Lord, every day
   I ask,

      and you give to me.
   I seek,

      and you provide the answers.
   I knock,

      and you open the door.

You are always there
      giving,

         providing,

            and opening.

Thank you Lord.

Thank you so very much!

My my Lord,

I felt like punching him

right in the mouth.

There I was trying to be helpful,

and he made a fool of me

in front of everyone.

The situation called for

the natural person to attack.

Anything less would appear cowardice.

But you said, "Turn the other cheek."

So I walked away.

Lord, it took guts to do that.

Help me to be as brave the next time.

Dear Lord God,

   the harder I try to lead a good life

   the harder the Devil tries to trip me up.

He constantly places temptations in my way

      and too often, he causes me to fall.

I struggle to escape temptation,

   but it frequently overcomes me.

Shattered, broken, and beaten,

   I sometimes think, "What's the use?"

Lord, I can't beat temptation alone.

      I need help . . . your help!

Guide me past Satan's enticing offers.

Keep me from stumbling,

   and hold me on that steady course

      which leads to an eternity with you.

Dear God,

If I were to be the recipient

of a heart or a brain,

I've often thought about whose

heart or brain I would choose.

I've decided that I would take

the heart and brain of a bigot.

Then I would have one

that has hardly ever been used.

But, Lord, how about my heart?

How about my brain?

May neither one become compromised

in the life I live among your people.

Singing Lord,

is one of the joys of life.

The Psalmist says,

"Oh sing to the Lord a new song,

for he has done marvelous things."

Many times when I raise my voice to you,

it must sound like the same old tune.

It is not a song of praise

for marvelous things done,

but it is that familiar chorus of

gripes and requests.

Help me to become more sensitive

to your marvelous deeds.

Help me compose a song –

a totally new song.

Almighty God,

    grant me the courage to hope,

the strength to persevere,

    and the faith to believe.

Help me to both love

    as I have been loved

and to forgive

    as I have been forgiven.

I call myself a Christian.

Grant that I may better become

    what I like to claim to be.

For without your help, Lord,

    I could never consider myself

        one of your own.

Of all people, Jesus,

a Roman Centurion made you marvel

over his faith.

Concerned about his paralyzed servant,

humbly he came,

convinced you could heal him.

Jesus, I bring before you my concerns.

I know that you can mend

my fractured existence.

All I need is the kind of faith

that also makes you marvel.

Grant it to me Lord!

Thank you, God.

Thank you for everything.

Even for little things like

    pens and combs and books.

Every good thing comes from your

    abundant hand.

But of all your goodness God,

    Jesus Christ is your finest gift.

There isn't enough time

    to sufficiently thank you for him.

Even an entire lifetime

    wouldn't even provide a beginning.

Hunger, Lord . . .

   hungry people, starving people,

   stomachs filled only with emptiness.

Problems, Lord . . .

   people with problems,

      people forgotten and homeless.

People, Lord . . .

   people with souls,

   people you died for,

   people you love,

   your people.

Help me Lord . . .

Help me hear the cries of your people.

   Help me to realize that caring for you

      also involves me caring for them.

Forgive me, Lord

   for what I have been.

Help me to see more clearly

   who I am.

Direct me

   to what I shall be.

Help me better realize that

   I am acceptable in your sight

      only because

you Christ were, are, and ever will be

   my Savior and Lord.

Young people, Jesus, are really great!

It's really too bad

    that the church often turns them off.

Being a member of the church,

    perhaps I am part of the problem.

It is not that they don't love you.

      They really do!

Viewing the church as irrelevant to them,

    they often absent themselves.

Help me to remember our youth

    before you in prayer.

Fill me with your power and presence

    so that both young and old

    will encounter you through me.

Lord God,

Can I truly weep with those who weep

    when I often cause the weeping?

The question I have to settle is not

    what I would do for you

        if I had more time and money.

Rather what will I do

    with the time and money that I have?

You do not inquire,

    "What will you do for me tomorrow?"

Instead, you ask,

    "What are you doing for me today?"

Help me to do today, Lord,

    what I was going to do tomorrow.

Spring, Lord,

    is a most beautiful time of the year.

I hear the Psalmist proclaim,

    "The heavens are telling the glory of
    God; and the firmament proclaims his
    handiwork."

For truly, Lord,

    in the blue skies,

        budding trees,

            and blooming flowers,

I see the magnificence of your creation.

Rejoicing that you placed me

        in such wonderful surroundings,

            I begin this day.

Almighty God,

Help me during my life

    not to live in isolation from you.

Times can become so hectic,

    and life so complicated,

that you sometimes are squeezed out.

Give me the discipline which makes

    worship a priority

        and daily prayer a necessity.

You have assured me that

    you are always with me.

May I never be so unwise

    to break contact.

Time is quite an important word, Jesus.

In Scripture, we read,

> "But when the fullness of time had come,
>> God sent forth his son,
>>> born of a woman . . ."

Lord, this was the beginning

> of many important times in your life.

Only thirty-three years later

> came your death

>> and resurrection time.

Lord, as I look back at these past times

>> and then forward to your return

>>> at the end of time,

keep me faithful, for I now stand

> in the present:

>> the time between the times.

THREE

THE DARKNESS GROWS LESS

Jesus,

I light the candles of the Advent Wreath.

As the darkness grows less,

    my thoughts are more and more

        on your birth.

Once again, I consider your coming

    with peace, joy, and hope.

Help me to always realize that

    Christmas is not mere ancient history

        but also current events.

Come, Lord Jesus.

Come into my life

in a dramatic way . . .

as dramatic as your first

coming into this world.

At this time of year,

I especially invite you into my home.

Remain with me

until the Heavenly Father

invites me into his.

Lord Jesus Christ,

The Christmas spirit grows in me

   more and more each day.

It is hard to determine the basis

   for this special Christmas feeling.

I suppose it's a mixture of

   customs and traditions that go back

      to my childhood.

Yet, Christmas is so much more than

   warm sentimentality.

It is joy and gladness over the birth

   of the Father's only Son.

This makes me happy.

This gives me and the whole world

   an occasion for celebration.

You, Jesus, are the true spirt of Christmas.

Jesus,

Every year Christmas springs upon me

with increasing rapidity.

It is very easy to get caught up

in the feverish hustle and bustle

of this time of year.

Yet, I pray in all the chaos that

I won't miss the beautiful message

that eternal life can now be mine

because of a crying baby

in a Bethlehem barn.

FOUR

A BABY CRIES – A WORLD LISTENS

Dearest Jesus,

Christmas is so warm and beautiful.

Bright lights shine throughout

    the community.

Homes are decorated;

    presents are wrapped.

Good feelings and love abound.

Bless me and those I love

    as we celebrate your birth.

Bless us as we sing the carols

    and retell the ancient story.

Bless us with inner peace

    and good-will to all men.

Baby Jesus,

On the Eve of your birth,

    I feel so good inside.

Cookies are prepared,

  presents are wrapped,

  and the Christmas tree is decorated.

More importantly, Jesus,

    churches are full,

      families are together,

    and people greet one another

      with pleasant smiles.

Jesus, I wouldn't trade tonight

  for any other night in the whole year.

How can I possibly thank you?

  Any attempt would wind-up

    merely as a faint echo.

Dearest Christ Child,

Silent nights remind me

   of that one holy night

      many years ago.

With my tongue bursting

   with praise

and my heart filled

   with peace,

I worship the Father

   for the miracle of your birth.

When trouble visits my life,

   grant me a silent night

      to help me again remember

   that you are always there for me.

Lord Jesus,

I remember that holy night of years ago,

    a baby cradled in loving young arms,

    the excitement and pain of birth past,

    the calm state of exhaustion set in.

I remember startled shepherds,

    an angel announcing

        the best of news,

    heavens filled with songs of praise,

        promises of peace,

        and good-will to all.

As I remember that night, Lord,

    I am overwhelmed with joy.

Your Father loved me by sending you.

    You loved me by coming.

Dearest Jesus,

at your birth, men from the East

began following a special star

which led them to Bethlehem.

There they worshipped you

with gifts of gold

and frankincense

and myrrh.

We too worship you at your birth

with gifts of praise

and thanksgiving

and gifts of love.

May our worship also earn us

the title of wise men.

Tonight Lord,

I will join millions in singing,

"Should auld acquaintance be forgot,

and never brought to mind?

Should auld acquaintance be forgot,

and auld lang syne."

May my remembrance of this past year

also bring another familiar song

to my lips:

"Praise God from whom all blessings flow,

Praise Him all creatures here below,

Praise Him above, Ye Heavenly Hosts,

Praise Father, Son, and Holy Ghost."

FIVE

THE ULTIMATE SACRIFICE

Good Lord,

one day you led Peter, James, and John

    up a mountain and revealed your glory.

Transfigured, your face shone like the sun,

    and your garments were white as light.

On that mountain your Father spoke,

"This is my Son, the Beloved; with him I
    am well pleased; listen to him."

Lord, help me to listen

so that I can once again follow you

    down the mountain

        back into the world.

I'm packed and I'm ready to go Jesus.

At your Transfiguration, I saw you

as the glorious Son of God.

Now I am ready to walk with you

to Jerusalem.

I know what awaits you there.

Even as I contemplate

your suffering and death,

my thoughts keep shifting

to Easter and your resurrection.

I'm not jumping the gun.

It's just that the suffering

would be unbearable

without also contemplating

the final outcome.

Lord Jesus,

    you and your Father

        created the world

    out of nothing.

    Many say, "wonderful."

Yes to be sure.

But your death, Lord,

    did something still more wonderful.

    It made a saint

        out of a sinner

            like me.

Almighty God,

    you showed us how to love

with the unselfish giving of your Son.

You told us that,

    "No one has greater love than this,

to lay down one's life for one's friends."

Some people are willing to go that far,

    most of us are not.

Each day, help me to give something

      of myself to others.

That way I might be ready,

    if I'm ever asked,

        to make the ultimate sacrifice.

Oh Lord,

The sound of hammer on nail

    continues to ring in my ears.

Slowly they raise you from the ground

    until the cross thumps into place.

There, suspended between

    heaven and earth

your life fulfills its purpose.

On the surface it looks like failure,

    but this is God's will.

What a horrible way to die!

To think you considered me worthy

    of such pain and agony,

    Lord, I'll never understand why.

But I know that your death

    made it a Good Friday for me.

Jesus,

I know that everyone who is born will die.

But you Lord were born to die.

  You came and died for us

      not because we deserved it,

         but because we needed it.

Scripture tells us that the greatest love

      we can show for another

      is to lay down our lives for them.

Honestly, Lord, It would be hard for me

      to be able to love quite that much.

As I survey your wondrous cross,

     may I not only feel loved

but also be motivated to love others

     as you have loved me.

SIX

THE ULTIMATE VICTORY

Triumphant Christ,

Your resurrection victory

    opened the gates of heaven

    exposing the Father's throne

        to all believers.

With colorful clothes, Easter lilies,

    many smiles, and packed churches,

        we proclaim to the world

    that we celebrate

        the victory of all victories,

    the death of all deaths

        and the gift of eternal life.

For this, we praise and thank you God!

Lord Jesus,

Your resurrection gives us eternal hope.

   The darkness of Good Friday passes.

The light of Easter morning appears.

I am thrilled, Lord,

   as I contemplate victory over death.

I know that my Redeemer lives

   and am comforted in knowing

      I can now live eternally as well.

Thanks and praise be to

   God the Father,

      and God the Son,

         and God the Holy Spirit.

Who loves me even beyond

   my highest hopes.

Death Lord,

is the one enemy I can never conquer.

Its action is always decisive.

I am never truly ready for it.

Lord your resurrection

did what I could never do.

It conquered death and the grave.

Since I believe in you,

death has lost its power over me.

With St. Paul, I can now revile death,

"Where, Oh death, is your victory?

Where, Oh death, is your sting?"

Lord, your resurrection abolished death

and gave me an eternal lease on life.

For this, I cannot thank you enough.

Resurrected Lord,

Not only has your resurrection

     provided me with eternal life

for which I am ever grateful,

     but you have promised me

resurrection power as I live for you.

Yes, Jesus, with you now living in me,

     I have the power to serve you

          in dynamic ways.

Help me to know

    how you wish me to work for you;

       then give me the courage to do it.

For with your power residing in me,

     I have nothing to fear.

SEVEN

COME HOLY SPIRIT

Holy Spirit,

At Pentecost you came smashing

   into this world.

Before long, you turned it upside down.

You used ordinary people like me

   to introduce others to Christ.

Before long, a lost world was changed.

Lord, give me the courage

   to invite the Spirit to use me.

For if I am not sharing you with others,

   I am depriving them of you.

On the surface, Lord,

    Christianity would seem much nicer

      if it were just personal.

But Jesus commands us to tell his story

      to the whole world.

James says that true religion

      also involves helping

         the hungry and the sick.

Sometimes I feel like Charlie Brown

      who concludes,

        "There is no problem so big that

        you can't run away from it."

May I realize that there is no such thing

      as an isolated Christian,

      for my neighbor has a claim on me.

Jesus,

Before your Ascension, you told your
followers to tell the whole world
about you.
You sent them the Holy Spirit
to provide the power to do this.

Today, things have not changed.
You still want me to share your love
with those I encounter.
And the same Spirit stands ready to help.

For if a man has a soul . . . and he has,
and if that soul can be won or lost for
eternity . . . and it can,
the most important thing in the world is
to tell that person about you.

EIGHT

CALLED BY NAME

Great God,

At Baptism you sunk

   your hooks into me.

You called me by name,

   and I became yours.

Sometimes I find myself

   wanting to break away.

But no matter how hard I try,

   you won't let me go.

You love me so much that

   you continually call me back.

Thank you for sticking by me

   even when loving me gets difficult.

Lord God,

The cry of a healthy baby

is a very beautiful sound.

It is especially beautiful

when the baby is your own.

After nine months of anxious anticipation,

you have blessed my wife and me

with a healthy child.

Lord, we can't thank you enough.

Already we look forward to her

becoming yours through Baptism.

May she grow up to give you glory.

Help us help her along the way.

Remember me dear Lord,

and help me to remember

that I am your child

through Baptism.

Give me the strength to overcome

the assaults of the Tempter.

And rescue me

whenever I begin to fall.

I put my trust in you, Lord.

We both know that the Devil

doesn't stand a chance

when you are firmly planted

in my heart.

Most of my prayers, Lord,

  are centered on me.

Today I am coming to you

  in behalf of others.

In Baptism, the concerns of others

  have also become my concerns,

    their problems, my problems.

For those who are spiritually sick,

  Lord make me your witness.

For those who grieve and are lonely,

  Lord, move me to comfort them.

Lord, I'll talk to you later

  about my own special needs.

For now, be with all the others,

  my brothers and sisters in Christ.

NINE

TWO BECOME ONE

Lord,

If Bill loves Carol,

    and Carol only loves Carol,

    who's going to love Bill?

If Carol loves Bill

    and Bill only loves Bill,

    who's going to love Carol.

Help Bill love Carol.

Help Carol love Bill.

This is the day, Lord.

   I have been looking forward

      to today for quite some time.

In just a few hours, I'll be pledging myself

      to love another person

         for richer, for poorer

      for better, for worse

         in sickness and in health

      'til death do us part.

This is certainly promising quite a lot,

      and I'll surely need your help.

You have promised to bless those

      who stand before you in marriage.

Thank you Lord for the blessing

      we are about to receive.

Good Lord,

I pray for the young couple just married.

Now as they begin life's journey,

   no longer as two individuals but as one,

may each new experience cause

  their love to increase.

Keep destructive temptation from them,

   and may nothing hurt their marriage.

In due time, bless them with children,

   so that their marriage will assume

     an even greater joy and meaning.

For young love,

     the blessings of marriage,

       and the gift of children,

I praise the holy name

    of our good Lord and God.

Dear Lord,

Two people plan

to become one

through marriage.

The wedding . . .

just two days away.

Frantic last minute preparations.

In all of the rush,

may they not forget that you are

the key to a long

and successful future.

Most merciful God,

Fifty years of marriage is a long time,

and it is also a great blessing.

We thank you for the blessing

of being together for so long.

More than this Lord, we want to thank you

for helping us bear many burdens

and for being with us when life was difficult.

You have given us wonderful children,

and you provided us material blessings.

Most importantly, you have loved us

and have given us forgiveness.

Because of this, we can look forward

to being with each other and you

for an eternity.

TEN

WHEN YOU ARE HURTING

Whatever is big enough to worry about

    is not too small to pray about.

I'm worried about all the tests I'm taking

    and what the doctors might find.

Lord, it is especially trying

    when you have an unknown illness.

Give me strength to face this ordeal

    with the least amount of strain.

Help me accept the outcome of these tests.

    Lord, instill in me the peace

    which comes from knowing you care.

Alone Lord,

    I feel alone, all alone.

        I really don't know why.

People love me; I have friends,

    but this awful feeling continues.

Why, Lord, why?

    I know you are always there.

My friends are ready and willing to help.

Could it be that I might be the problem?

    Maybe, Lord, I don't want to be loved,

        for then I would have to love in return.

You can't love and be loved

    and still feel alone.

Lord,

You tell me to pray without ceasing

    and to cast all my cares on you.

I was hurting last week

    so I prayed to you often.

You heard my prayers,

    demonstrated your love,

        and met my needs.

 Now I am so much better.

You care.

    Prayer works.

        Thanks Lord.

My dear Lord,

thank you for helping my friend

during his delicate operation.

He is your servant and loves you dearly.

I join the prayers of many on his behalf.

During his recovery, may his pain be mild

and may his spirits be high.

He is anxious to return to his family.

They are anxious to have him back.

Grant him a speedy recovery.

During sickness,

people especially need friends.

Help me to be a really good one for him.

God of love and healing,

    friends have asked me to pray

        for their very sick child.

The situation is touch and go

    and even the doctors are worried.

Naturally Lord,

    we are all praying for a miracle.

And we completely trust

    in your ability to perform one.

Therefore, we simply ask

    that you heal her.

Now we put the matter

    completely in your hands, Lord,

        knowing that it couldn't be

        in a better place.

Dearest Jesus,

    you know how much I was troubled

        when I visited Mary last week.

Such a beautiful person and so crippled.

    It is hard, so really hard for me

        to accept this tragedy.

Recently, she made a great improvement.

    Mary can now talk and feed herself.

She was so happy and proud that

    after 13 years, she can do this again.

And she loves her family's weekly visits.

Lord, if life ever crashes in on me,

    help me to be content with

        simple things . . .

    talking, feeding myself,

        and weekly family visits.

Dear Father in Heaven,

   sickness is a time of special need.

When I am sick, I also feel afraid.

I wonder deep down inside

   if things will ever be the same.

Will I get well, return home,

   fulfill my dreams?

Father, where doubt now resides

   fill my heart with trust.

I know that I can carry

   great and heavy burdens

      as long as I don't try

         to carry them all alone.

Dear God Almighty,

    you hold in your hands life and death

        and all points in between.

Today I am sick, really sick.

I simply want to cry out, "Heal me, God!"

It is hard for me to accept sickness –

    especially my own.

Help me understand that you can

    even use suffering and sickness

        to draw me closer to you.

I would never ask for sickness, Lord,

    but now that I'm sick,

        help me to find a blessing

            even in it.

Good Lord,

I always have time for you

    when I have problems.

Sickness, death, and discouragement

    force me to my knees crying for help.

And then when you answer my prayers,

I once again put you back

    on my spiritual medicine shelf

        until the next crisis.

How foolish of me!

You are not a part-time God.

You want to be involved in my life

    every moment of every day.

My daily life will be more abundant

    if I invite you into it.

Help me to wise-up, Lord.

Good Lord,

Little Peter was hit by a car.

He is so young in a strange hospital.

Lord, this little boy is lonesome and afraid.

His parents are frustrated that

      they can't do more for their child.

They also feel guilty that they left him alone

      that one critical moment.

Lord, heal Peter so he can go home.

Comfort him and his parents

      while they are separated.

Grant that something good might result

      from all of this sadness.

Deliver, me Lord,

    from evil:

the evil in the world

    that tempts me to do wrong

and that part of me

    which finds it so attractive.

Give me strength to overcome evil

    and the power to do your will.

Don't abandon me for even a minute.

For if I am left alone,

    I will reap only destruction.

Lord, war makes me sick . . .

    it has claimed the lives

        of far too many people.

Today, I learned that my friend

    has become part of the tragedy.

It's tough, really tough

    to swallow the bitter pill

    of the death of a fine young man.

At times, the pain seems unbearable.

Once again, I pray for peace.

    Give the world that peace the angels
      sang about so long ago.

A peace that covers the earth

    and fosters good-will among

      all God's people everywhere.

ELEVEN

ETERNITY WITH GOD

Heaven, Lord,

It is your special gift to all who believe.

    Thank you for such a wonderful gift.

Because of Jesus' life, death,

    and resurrection,

      heaven moved from a mere dream

        to a certain truth.

Keep me strong in my faith,

for there is nothing which I desire more

then as my last earthy breath moves

    from my lungs through my mouth

      that heaven will become

        my forever reality.

O dearest Jesus,

    my heart is so sad tonight.

The words, "Christine was killed,"

    continually flood my mind.

Lord, the tragedy of it all

    is most difficult to understand.

Only four-years-old,

    she was a happy, beautiful child.

If words could bring her back,

    I would gladly speak them.

One day, Lord, you encouraged

    the little ones to come to you.

Today Christine came.

    Comfort me.

      Take care of her.

Dear Lord God,

in your wise judgment

and with his best interest at heart,

you called my best friend

to his everlasting home.

Thank you for making him yours

through the gift of Baptism.

For the Word that strengthened his faith

and the sacraments that forgave his sins,

I offer my sincere thanks.

But Lord, his gain is my loss.

Comfort me as I mourn his death.

In this my time of grief,

reach out your arms and hold me.

Keep my faith strong so that one day

I'll too come home to you and to him.

Giver of life and death,

thank you for taking my loved one home,

    for she was in so much pain.

She now rests after a life filled

    with much joy and many sorrows.

As I rejoice over her crown of victory,

I am also experiencing so much pain –

    pain of loss, separation,

        hopes smashed,

            and plans unfulfilled.

She learned to handle the truth

    that she must die.

Help me learn to handle the void

    that her death creates.

My dear Savior,

    may I never forget

        that growing old is a privilege

           denied to so very many.

Thank you for the many wonderful years

    you have allowed me to live.

 Now that I am old and my body is worn,

    I find pain a constant companion

and bad days outnumbering the good.

This life is becoming more difficult,

    and I find myself thinking

        more and more about the next.

When death finally comes my way,

help me to welcome it and say,

    "Lord, I am ready to go home,

      please lead the way."

TWELVE

PRAISE AND THANKSGIVING

Too often Lord,

    my prayers are only about

        my wants and my needs.

I sometimes forget that you also desire

    my regular thanks and praise.

Today I praise your holy name

    God of all creation and

        Lord of everything good.

Help me to daily remember

    to be thankful to you in all things.

May I regularly praise you with

    my words and with my actions.

Spectacular and amazing God,

>your wonders fill the earth.

Your kindness is without equal.

Goodness flows from your very being.

Your love is broad and deep enough

>to even include me in its sphere.

Not deserving it but needing it,

>I am forever in your debt.

I thank you for being my God.

I thank you for loving me as I am.

And I thank you for hanging in with me

>especially when I am less than

>you desire me to be.

Gracious Lord,

all that I am and might be emanates

out of your love for me.

Thank you for loving me so completely.

I love you too Lord,

but my love for you is only a mere

approximation of your love for me.

For you loved me to death . . .

the death of your beloved Son.

Knowing that I am incapable of loving as

deeply as I have been loved,

help me Lord to at least approximate it.

Accept my imperfect love for others,

for it is the best I can give.

God of glory,

all creation displays the brilliance

    of your handiwork.

From daybreak to setting sun,

    beauty enhances our lives.

How blessed we are to behold your glory.

Thank you Lord for every flower and animal,

    for each in its own way worships you.

Every day you bless us with sights and

    sounds that bring us joy.

With each new breath we draw,

    your genius amazes us.

May we never take these gifts for granted

    . . . not even for a moment.

Thank you Lord for my yesterdays.

Thank you Lord for my tomorrows.

But yesterday is history and tomorrow

is a gift that only you

can decide to give me.

So mostly, Lord,

I wish to thank you for today.

Since I will only have one opportunity

to live today well, grant that

I live today to its fullest.

May my words and my actions please you

and bring honor to your name.

And may the way I live today

bring a smile to your face.

You, Oh Lord, are worthy of my daily praise.

By your grace, I have been gifted

with life itself.

And through your mercy,

I have been assured

of an eternal future.

God, how can I ever thank you enough?

Even my entire lifetime

is not adequate.

Grant me heaven Lord,

so that I might join your angels

in eternal praise

and thanksgiving.

About the Author

John Krahn has been a pastor for nearly fifty years. He pastored the largest multi-staffed Lutheran church in New York for eighteen years. Currently he is working as a church consultant specializing in stewardship and evangelism. He is a prolific writer. During his long ministry, he has been the CEO of a Lutheran social service agency, an Army Chaplain, the Director of Admissions at a Lutheran high school, an Interim Pastor at several churches, and owned his own business. He is also a much published author and sought-after speaker.

Krahn holds a Doctorate in Divinity Degree from New York Theological Seminary, New York; a Masters in Divinity Degree from Concordia Seminary, St. Louis; a Master's Degree in Theological Studies from Union Seminary, New York; a Master's Degree in Education from Columbia University, New York; and a Bachelor of Arts Degree from Concordia Senior College, Indiana.

Krahn is married with two children and three grandchildren. He believes that our God who is behind us is greater than the challenges which are before us.